Room Behavior

Rob Kovitz

Treyf Books
keep refrigerated

INSOMNIAC PRESS

Canadian Cataloguing in Publication Data

Kovitz, Rob, 1963-
    Room behavior

ISBN 1-895837-44-8

1. Rooms - Psychological aspects.
2. Architecture - Human factors.
3. Human behaviour. I. Title.

NA2540.K68   1997   720'.1'9   C96-932447-2

Design & production by Rob Kovitz & Mike O'Connor

Readied for the press by Kirsty Adam

Printed and bound in Canada

Insomniac Press
378 Delaware Ave.
Toronto, Ontario, Canada, M6H 2T8

Room Behavior

"By coming in here, you agree to a certain behavior," Mink said.
"What behavior?"
"Room behavior."

Don DeLillo, White Noise

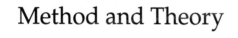

Method and Theory

He was entering a room. Most stately. Nothing to be alarmed. Faces watched him through the smoke. Must nod to each. Appear plausible.

Cormac McCarthy, Suttree

The seating arrangement at both kitchen and dining-room tables was rigidly adhered to. Dale always sat on the north end of both the dinette and diningroom tables. Jenny sat on the northwest side of the round dinette table and on the east side of the rectangular dining-room table. Bob sat on the east side of the dinette table and the west side of the dining-room table. Linda sat on the west side of the dinette table and south side of the dining-room table. The dining-room table was usually used only for Sunday dinner, or when there were guests.

Susan Kent, Analysing Activity Areas: An Ethnoarcheological Study of the Use of Space

The decision of the room is a commitment. It is an old and venerable tradition. One which cannot be taken lightly.

Eldon Garnet, I Shot Mussolini

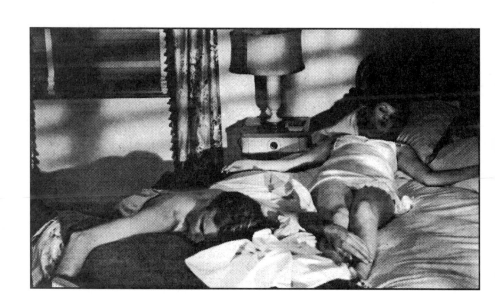

In the room there is the air
                              and there is the corner
and there is the corner and there is the corner
and there is the corner.

If you don't shake, don't get no cake.

Michael Ondaatje, Coming Through Slaughter

Euroamerican Spatial Patterning

She stood back from the door and I went past her into a square room with a minimum of uninteresting furniture. A small lamp on a window table made a dim yellowish light. The window behind it was open.

"Sit down," she said, shutting the door.

I sat down.

Raymond Chandler, The Lady in the Lake

During the daytime Gregor did not want to show himself at the window, out of consideration for his parents, but he could not crawl very far around the few square yards of floor space he had, nor could he bear lying quietly at rest all during the night, while he was fast losing any interest he had ever taken in food, so that for mere recreation he had formed the habit of crawling crisscross over the walls and ceiling. He especially enjoyed hanging suspended from the ceiling; it was much better than lying on the floor; one could breathe more freely; one's body swung and rocked lightly; and in the almost blissful absorption induced by this suspension it could happen to his own surprise that he let go and fell plump on the floor.

Franz Kafka, The Metamorphosis

I don't like bathrooms. I don't bathe as a habit. I've had baths in my time, but I prefer to wash or shower. Since I was a child in the war, and my father was what one might describe as a glutton for austerity, and any kind of privation that the government recommended one should indulge in he leapt upon with great glee. On our bath at home he fixed a knot in the chain of the plug which suggested the recommended level the bath should be, which just about covered an eighth of a buttock. Since I was the youngest in the family, I was the last to bathe — we shared the same bath water — so by the time I got around and my filthy brother had finished, there wasn't much left for me — my father hadn't added anything to it — so the whole idea of the bathroom is associated to me with bleakness and discomfort.

Peter Greenaway, 26 Bathrooms

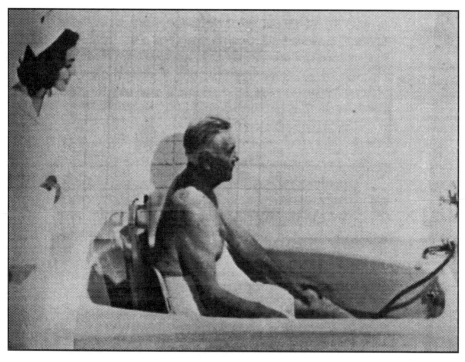

Joseph F. Schram, Planning and Remodeling a Bathroom

She took to sitting for hours each day in the darkened boiler-room of the orphanage. She told Esther, her sister, that she did this because she could feel herself splitting into pieces, evaporating in the daylight. The darkness left her intact.

Eric McCormack, The Paradise Motel

The point of rooms is that they're inside. No one should go into a room unless he understands this. People behave one way in rooms, another way in streets, parks and airports. To enter a room is to agree to a certain kind of behavior. It follows that this would be the kind of behavior that takes place in rooms. This is the standard, as opposed to parking lots and beaches. It is the point of rooms.

Don DeLillo, White Noise

Hostess plays follow the leader with 3 girls and 2 boys. They run, jump, hop, clap and wave hands and arms, then they go back to their chairs.

F. Earle Barcus, Romper Room: An Analysis

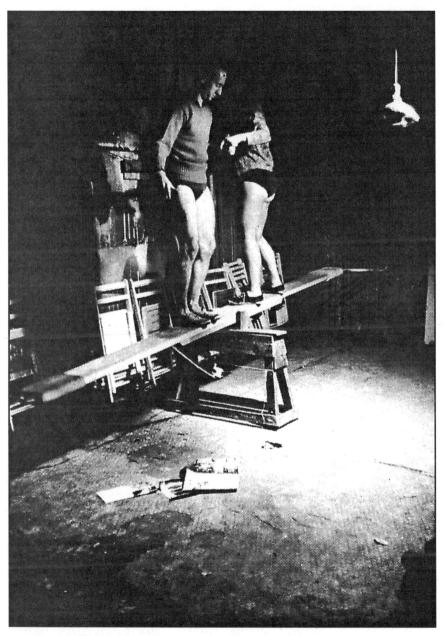

Simone Forti, See-Saw

Living Rooms

A quick memory. I was four years old, sitting quietly on the couch of my family's living room, waiting for the world to commence.

B.W. Powe, Outage

K. Luchesskoy, Housing to Fit the Need

In the familiar darkness of his room, Gordon felt for the gas-jet and lighted it. The room was medium-sized, not big enough to be curtained into two, but too big to be sufficiently warmed by one defective oil-lamp. It had the sort of furniture you expect in a top floor back. White-quilted single bed; brown lino floor-covering; wash-hand-stand with jug and basin of that cheap white ware which you can never see without thinking of chamberpots. On the window-sill there was a sickly aspidistra in a green-glazed pot.

George Orwell, Keep the Aspidistra Flying

Furniture by L. Reich, 1931

"It's so dirty," she said in her husky voice. "I hate clean rooms. I hate people who are always afraid of leaving a trail. That's why this place is wonderful. You live here and you leave your marks, and after you stay long enough it's going to be in the walls, and the air, and a part of you is never going to leave here."

Norman Mailer, Barbary Shore

The room is not only the universe but also the etui of the private person. To live means to leave traces. In the room these are emphasized.

Walter Benjamin

Know most of the rooms of thy native country before thou goest over the threshold thereof.

Thomas Fuller, The Holy State and the Profane State

Vasari Junior, La Pietra, anteroom with frescoed walls

Rose: This is a nice room.

Harold Pinter, The Room

(They place you in a room, and they make you describe it.)

It is the way the windows are always dirty. Spattered, a black film of car exhaust. Drips of pigeon shit. Dead bugs in the ripped screen. When you look out this is what you see. It makes you sick. You will remove the panes of filthy glass, and then you will clean them. There is nothing to stop you from doing this. But you do not do it. You could not possibly do it, you can barely move. This is it. Or a part of it.

Daniel Jones, Obsessions

A certain number of walls are one of the necessary evils of the business. And while some of you will understandably bridle at the expense, the observant student is aware that walls offer a good return on investment by way of providing one of the basic components of rooms.

Fran Lebowitz, A Manual: Training for Landlords

Leon woke in the white rectangular room in which he lived. He stared at the blank walls in a quiet panic until sleepiness fell away.

Robert Boswell, The Geography of Desire

Alvar Aalto, Paimio Sanitorium, 1929-31.

The old man lived in a long, narrow white room, with a ceiling resembling the lid of a coffin. A wide window shone dimly opposite the door. A little stove stood in the corner to the left of the entrance. A bed extended along the left wall, and opposite it sprawled a sagging reddish sofa. The room smelled strongly of camphor and dried herbs. The old man opened the window, and heaved a deep sigh.

Maxim Gorky, The Life of a Useless Man

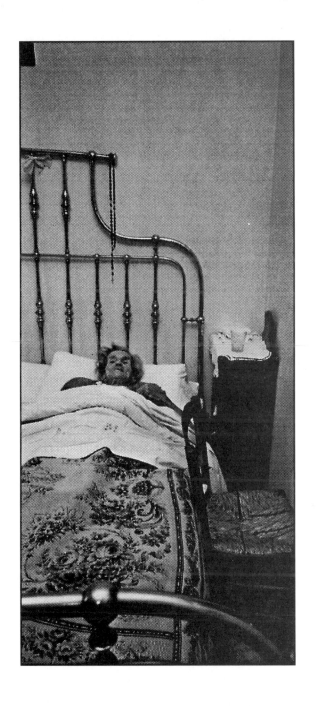

Perhaps being old is having lighted rooms
Inside your head, and people in them, acting.
People you know, yet can't quite name.

Philip Larkin, The Old Fools

A room is like a violin. One can get to know a violin by practicing on it, a room by living in it.

Adolf Loos, Interiors in the Rotunda

all I want is a room, I said. it's very cold. I'll pay you. I may not have enough for a week but I just want to get out of the cold. it's not dying that's bad, it's being lost that's bad.

Charles Bukowski, Notes of a Dirty Old Man

Matthew Geller, Difficulty Swallowing

On reaching my room I'll feel warm, I'll light the lamp in its iron stand on my table, and when I've done that I'll lie back in my armchair which stands on the torn Oriental carpet. Pleasant prospects! Why not? But then? No then. The lamp will shine in the warm room, shine on my chest as I lie in the armchair. Then I'll cool off and spend hours alone between the painted walls and the floor which, reflected in the mirror hanging on the rear wall, appears slanted.

Franz Kafka, Description of a Struggle

Rose: Well, Mr Kidd, I must say this is a very nice room. It's a very comfortable room.
Mr. Kidd: Best room in the house.
Rose: It must get a bit damp downstairs.
Mr. Kidd: Not as bad as upstairs.
Rose: What about downstairs?
Mr. Kidd: Eh?
Rose: What about downstairs?
Mr. Kidd: What about it?
Rose: Must get a bit damp.
Mr. Kidd: A bit. Not as bad as upstairs though.
Rose: Why's that?
Mr. Kidd: The rain comes in.

Harold Pinter, The Room

Small rooms, large rooms, dark rooms, rooms elegant and luminous with age. I was searching for something — I didn't know what: Not a study, not a workroom, not a living room; just a room someone had lived in before me, the man I wanted to become.

Robert Musil, The Man Without Qualities.

Lewis Klahr, Deep Fishtank, Too

He shall shew you a large upper room furnished: there make ready.

Luke 22:12

How to Work a Room

I go there and I sit in her room, and we are very quiet, I don't fucking camp around, I never smoke, and we tell one another the truth.

Julian Barnes, Talking it Over

Ralph Levy, Bedtime Story

The purpose of a room derives from the special nature of a room. A room is inside. This is what people in rooms have to agree on, as differentiated from lawns, meadows, fields, orchards.

Don DeLillo, White Noise

Billy Wilder, Double Indemnity

Very soon, Krantz, very soon I'm going to be in a room with her.
We're going to be in a room. There's going to be a room around us.

Leonard Cohen, The Favourite Game

Then Lucy's voice said, "What are you having for lunch?"

"I've got my mother's meatloaf sandwiches," I said, climbing down from the chair.

"Why don't you eat them in my room, in style?"

At her room, I showed her how the meatloaf just dripped out of the sandwich if I tilted the bread. A crumbly hunk of wet hamburger slid into a pool of ketchup on the plate.

Lucy said, "Some people think it's more polite to say catsup."

The room was too small to hold a table. It was a little cube for living in. She told me it was perfect for one person.

"This is my garden," she said, showing me the flower pots on the window sill — African violets, and geraniums, and herbs such as mint and thyme. "This is my bed — as you know," she said. "And this is my library" — a bookshelf with about fifty paperbacks jammed onto it. She showed me where she kept her letters ("My extensive files") and where she hid her money ("My bank"). Her kitchen was a shelf with a hotplate and some cans of soup, and her clothes were in a shallow closet. All these things she showed me by stretching out her hand. It was such a tiny room I could not move without knocking something over. Just being there with her was like a sexual act.

Paul Theroux, My Secret History

Jean-Jacques Lequeu, Design of a Bed for the Beglierbey of Rumelia

Suttree peered into an old boudoir with mattresses along the walls. Tattered grey army blankets. A thin little man was squatting by the window masturbating. He did not take his eyes from Suttree nor did he cease pulling at his limp and wattled cock. It was deadly cold in the room.

Cormac McCarthy, Suttree

Actually, to my surprise, her living room was not in execrable taste. The furniture was modest, but she had achieved some decent effects. A mattress and spring on legs was covered by a dark green spread and served as a couch. There were several old armchairs with new print materials, and a dull tan rug was set against tomato-colored drapes. There were more mirrors than she needed upon the wall, the lamps were shabby, and needless gewgaws were clustered upon every end table, but altogether one could notice a certain unity.

"This is a nice room," I told her.

Norman Mailer, Barbary Shore

Maurice Defrène, Woman's Bedroom, Exposition des Arts Décoratifs, Paris, 1925

"Another thing I liked about your place was that it was filthy. Beer bottles all over the floor. Lots of trash everywhere. Dirty dishes, and a shit-ring in your toilet, and the crud in your bathtub. All those rusty razorblades laying around the bathroom sink. I knew that you would eat pussy."

"You judge a man according to his surroundings, right?"

Charles Bukowski, Women

Look around the room. Observe the situation. What is happening? Does there seem to be a good crowd? Do they seem to be enjoying themselves? Was the traffic or the parking difficult? What do these people have in common?

Susan Roane, How to Work a Room

No one should enter a room not knowing the point. There is an unwritten agreement between the person who enters a room and the person whose room has been entered, as opposed to open-air theaters, outdoor pools.

Don DeLillo, White Noise

She called me a filthy name.

I didn't mind that. I didn't mind what she called me, what anybody called me. But this was the room I had to live in. It was all I had in the way of a home. In it was everything that was mine, that had any association for me, any past, anything that took the place of a family. Not much; a few books, pictures, radio, chessmen, old letters, stuff like that. Nothing. Such as they were they had all my memories.

I couldn't stand her in that room any longer. What she called me only reminded me of that.

I said carefully: "I'll give you three minutes to get dressed and out of here. If you're not out by then, I'll throw you out — by force. Just the way you are, naked. And I'll throw your clothes after you into the hall. Now — get started."

Her teeth chattered and the hissing noise was sharp and animal. She swung her feet to the floor and reached for her clothes on a chair beside the bed. She dressed. I watched her. She dressed with stiff awkward fingers — for a woman — but quickly at that. She was dressed in a little over two minutes. I timed it.

She stood there for a moment and hissed at me, her face still like scraped bone, her eyes empty and yet full of some jungle emotion. Then she walked quickly to the door and opened it and went out, without speaking, without looking back. I heard the elevator lurch into motion and move in the shaft.

I walked to the windows and pulled the shades up and opened the windows wide. The night air came drifting in with a kind of stale sweetness that still remembered automobile exhausts and the streets of the city. I reached for my drink and drank it slowly. The apartment house door closed itself down below me. Steps tinkled on the quiet sidewalk. A car started up not far away. It rushed off into the night with a rough clashing of gears. I went back to the bed and looked down at it. The imprint of her head was still in the pillow, of her small corrupt body still on the sheets.

I put my empty glass down and tore the bed to pieces savagely.

Raymond Chandler, The Big Sleep

Marcel Breuer, Man's Room, Salon des Artistes Décorateurs, Paris, 1930

"It's characteristic," I said. "Pleasantly anarchical." Meaning the room.

Martin Amis, London Fields

Rose: Never mind about the room? What do you know about this room? You know nothing about it. And you won't be staying in it long either. My luck. I get these creeps come in, smelling up my room. What do you want?

Harold Pinter, The Room

The Mediascape, The Information Spew, Images Emanating Into Dark Rooms

In the renovated basement of her parents' home, we lay in each other's arms, clothed and warm and relaxed, on a brown leather couch. The TV gleamed.

"Jesus, TV makes me want to fuck," she said.

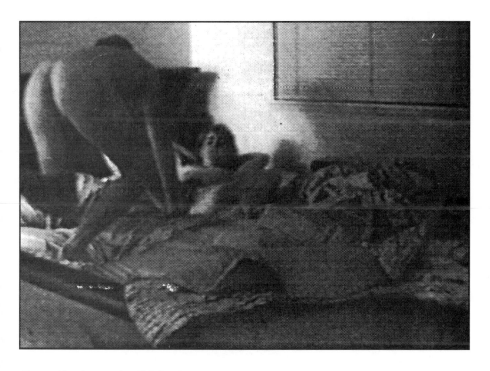

Tonya Harding and Jeff Gillooly, Home Video

And so the protean element we called electromagnetism had stolen indoors, subtly and deeply into the living room and basement, the den and kitchen and bedroom, impressing our senses and sensitivities, affecting what was forming in the slippery center of our private selves.

Hostess hands out 5 Romper Room punching clowns. Children get in circle and hit the punching clowns accompanied by musical record designed for this play.

F. Earle Barcus, Romper Room: An Analysis

Sorel Cohen, After Bacon/Muybridge, coupled figures/shoulder toss.

"Television," Christine murmured, "does something weird to me."

Programs teemed. Light was cast over the room.

B.W. Powe, Outage: A Journey Into Electric City

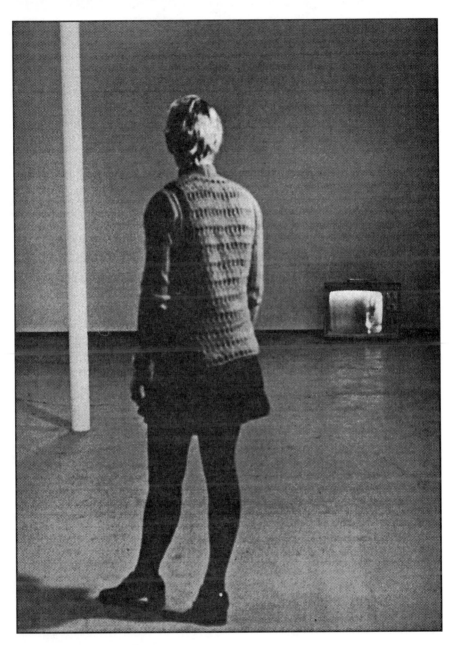

Bruce Nauman, Come Piece

How to Work a Room (II)

You put a man in a room and lock the door. There's something serenely pure here.

Don DeLillo, Mao II

Albrecht Dürer, Saint Jerome in his cell, 1514.

Take Hawthorne. After he graduated from college, he went back to his mother's house in Salem, shut himself up in his room, and didn't come out for twelve years.

Paul Auster, Ghosts

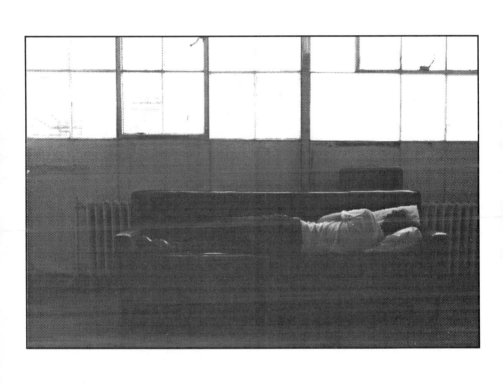

Pushed into an unlighted room, the door banged and locked for ever, I shall then have to light a lamp of aggressive voltage in my mind to keep at bay the night.

Wyndham Lewis

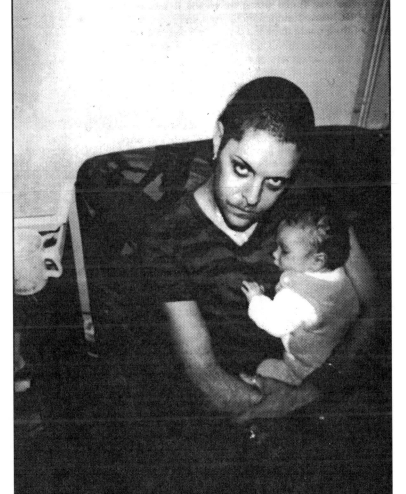

S. lived in a room so small that at first it seemed to defy you, to resist being entered. The presence of one person crowded the room, two people choked it. It was impossible to move inside it without contracting your mind to some infinitely small point within itself. Only then could you begin to breathe, to feel the room expand, and to watch your mind explore the excessive, unfathomable reaches of that space. For there was an entire universe in that room, a miniature cosmology that contained all that is most vast, most distant, most unknowable. It was a shrine, hardly bigger than a body, in praise of all that exists beyond the body: the representation of one man's inner world, even to the slightest detail. S. had literally managed to surround himself with the things that were inside him. The room he lived in was a dream space, its walls were like the skin of some second body around him, as if his own body had been transformed into a mind, a breathing instrument of pure thought. This was the womb, the belly of the whale, the original site of the imagination. By placing himself in that darkness, S. had invented a way of dreaming with open eyes.

Paul Auster, The Invention of Solitude

And women have sat indoors all these millions of years, so that by this time the very walls are permeated by their creative force.

Virginia Woolf, A Room of One's Own

Julien Duvivier, Flesh and Fantasy

I sat in my room like a spider. You've seen my hovel, haven't you? And do you realize, Sonia, that low ceilings and small, poky little rooms warp both mind and soul? Oh, how I loathed that hovel of mine! And yet I wouldn't leave it. Wouldn't leave it on purpose. Didn't go out for days. Didn't want to work. Didn't want to eat even. Just lay about. If Nastasya happened to bring me something, I'd eat; if not, a whole day would pass without my tasting anything. I wouldn't ask for anything deliberately, out of spite. At night I had no light, so I would lie in the dark. Didn't even try to earn enough money to buy myself a candle. I ought to have studied, but I sold my books; and on my table my notebooks are even now covered with dust an inch thick. I liked most of all to lie about and think. And I went on thinking. And I'd have such queer dreams, awful dreams, all sorts of dreams — I needn't tell you the kind of dreams they were.

Fyodor Dostoyevsky, Crime and Punishment

And these — the dreams — writhed in and about, taking hue from the rooms.

Edgar Allan Poe, The Masque of the Red Death

Alberto Giacometti, Annette, sitting

then I found a room outside the Village. for the looks and size of the room it was very cheap and I couldn't understand why. I found a bar around the corner and sipped at beers all day. my money was going but, as usual, I hated to look for a job. each drunken and starvation moment contained some type of easy meaning for me. that night I bought two bottles of port wine and went up to my room. I took off my clothes, got into bed in the dark, found a glass and poured the first wine. then I found why the room was so cheap. the 'L' ran right past my window. and that's where the stop was. right outside my window. the whole room would be lit by the train. and I'd look at a whole trainload of faces. horrible faces: whores, orangutans, bastards, madmen, killers — all my masters. then, swiftly the train would start up and the room would be dark again — until the next trainload of faces.

Charles Bukowski, Notes of a Dirty Old Man

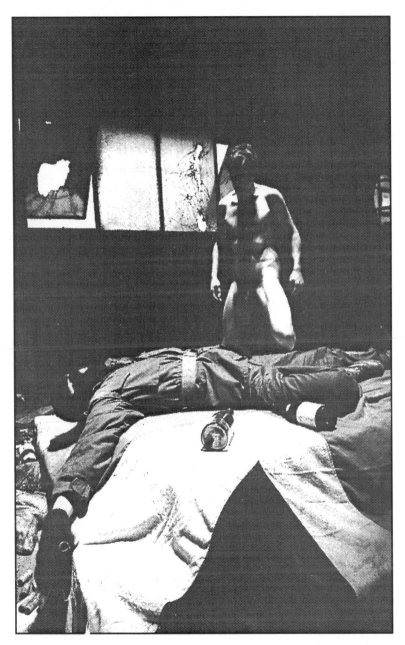

Derek Jarman, The Last of England

It takes, unhappily, no more than a desk and writing supplies to turn any room into a confessional. This may have nothing to do with the acts we have committed, or the humours we do go in and out of. It may be only the room, having no persuasive powers of its own. The room simply is. To occupy it, and find a metaphor there for memory, is our own fault.

Let me describe the room. The room measures 17 by 11 1/2 by 7 feet. The walls are lath and plaster, and painted the same shade of grey as were the decks of His Majesty's corvettes during the war. The room is oriented so that its diagonals fall NNE/SSW, and NW/SE.

One enters from the WSW, by a door midway in a long wall of the room. Standing just inside the door and turning clockwise one sees a portable wood stove in the NNE corner, surrounded by boxes, bowls, sacks containing food; the mattress, located halfway along the long ENE wall; a slop bucket in the SE corner; a washbasin in the SSW corner; a window facing the Dockyard; the door one has just entered; and finally in the NW corner, a small writing table and chair. The chair faces the WSW wall; so that the head must be turned 135 degrees to the rear in order to have a line-of-sight with the city. The walls are unadorned, the floor is carpetless. A dark grey stain is located on the ceiling directly over the stove.

That is the room. To say the mattress was begged from the Navy B.O.Q. here in Valletta shortly after the war, the stove and food supplied by CARE, or the table from a house now rubble and covered by earth; what have these to do with the room? The facts are history, and only men have histories. The facts call up emotional responses, which no inert room has ever showed us.

Why? Why use the room as an introduction to an apologia? Because the room, though windowless and cold at night, is a hothouse. Because the room is the past, though it has no history of its own. Because, as the physical being-there of a bed or horizontal plane determines what we call love; as a high place must exist before God's word can come to a flock and any sort of religion begin; so must there be a room...

Thomas Pynchon, V

... mind thriving in abstract idealist regions, freed from flesh. And room: the word links with rumor ...

Kika Thorne, Goodbye Suicide Girl.

... frequent mentions of the name "Romper Room" ...

Douglas Sirk, All That Heaven Allows

Only shallow people insist on disbelief. You and I know better. We understand how reality is invented. A person sits in a room and thinks a thought and it bleeds out into the world.

Don DeLillo, Mao II

The room. Brief mention of the room and/or the dangers lurking inside it. As in the image: Holderlin in his room.

For thirty-six years, fully half his life, he lived alone in the tower built for him by Zimmer, the carpenter from Tubingen — zimmer, which in German means room.

During those years, it is said, Holderlin rarely went out. When he did leave his room, it was only to take aimless walks through the country-side, filling his pockets with stones and picking flowers, which he would later tear to shreds.

Once, when a visitor was slow to leave his room, he showed him the door and said, with a finger raised in warning, "I am the Lord God."

In recent years there has been renewed speculation about Holderlin's life in that room. One man contends that Holderlin's madness was feigned, and that in response to the stultifying political reaction that overwhelmed Germany following the French revolution, the poet withdrew from the world. He lived, so to speak, underground in the room. According to this theory, all of the writings of Holderlin's madness (1806-1843) were in fact composed in a secret, revolutionary code.

Paul Auster, The Invention of Solitude

Quiet and co-operative. Fully oriented. Receives morning paper. Stays in his room most of the time.

While in room constantly hums.

Humphrey Carpenter, A Serious Character: A Life of Ezra Pound

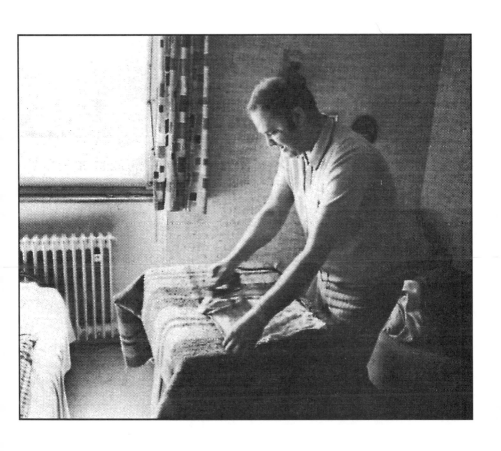

he goes through a book. photographs of poets mostly. I am not in there. I began late and lived too long alone in small rooms drinking wine. they always figure that a hermit is insane.

Charles Bukowski, Notes of a Dirty Old Man

He perches on the table:

Mrs. Sands: You're sitting down!
Mr. Sands (jumping up): Who is?
Mrs. Sands: You were.
Mr. Sands: Don't be silly. I perched.
Mrs. Sands: I saw you sit down.
Mr. Sands: You did not see me sit down because I did not sit bloody well down. I perched!
Mrs. Sands: Do you think I can't perceive when someone's sitting down?
Mr. Sands: Perceive! That's all you do. Perceive.
Mrs. Sands: You could do with a bit more of that instead of all that tripe you get up to.

Harold Pinter, The Room

Vito Acconci, Step Piece

There is reason, it is said, in the roasting of eggs, and there is philosophy even in furniture.

Edgar Allan Poe, Philosophy of Furniture

Wittgenstein's room, Trattenbach

All the unhappiness of man stems from one thing only, that he is incapable of staying quietly in his room.

Pascal

Van Gogh to his brother: "This time it is just simply my bedroom. To look at the picture ought to rest the brain or rather the imagination. The walls are pale violet. The floor is red tiles. The wood of the bed and chairs is the yellow of fresh butter, the sheet and pillows very light lemon-green. The coverlet scarlet. The window green. The toilet-table orange, the basin blue. The doors lilac. And that is all — there is nothing in this room with closed shutters. This by way of revenge for the enforced rest I have been obliged to take. I will make you sketches of the other rooms too some day."

Van Gogh, The Bedroom

As A. continued to study the painting, however, he could not help feeling that Van Gogh had done something quite different from what he thought he had set out to do. A.'s first impression was indeed a sense of calm, of "rest," as the artist describes it. But gradually, as he tried to inhabit the room presented on the canvas, he began to experience it as a prison, an impossible space, an image, not so much of a place to live, but of the mind that has been forced to live there. Observe carefully. The bed blocks one door, a chair blocks the other door, the shutters are closed: you can't get in, and once you are in, you can't get out. Stifled among the furniture and everyday objects of the room, you begin to hear a cry of suffering in this painting, and once you hear it, it does not stop. But there is no answer to this cry. The man in this painting (and this is a self-portrait, no different from a picture of a man's face, with eyes, nose, lips, and jaw) has been alone too much, has struggled too much in the depths of solitude. The world ends at that barricaded door. For the room is not a representation of solitude, it is the substance of solitude itself. And it is a thing so heavy, so unbreatheable, that it cannot be shown in any terms other than what it is. "And that is all — there is nothing in this room with closed shutters..."

Paul Auster, The Invention of Solitude

For myself, I can't think of anything in the world that is better than a nice room.

Gustave Flaubert

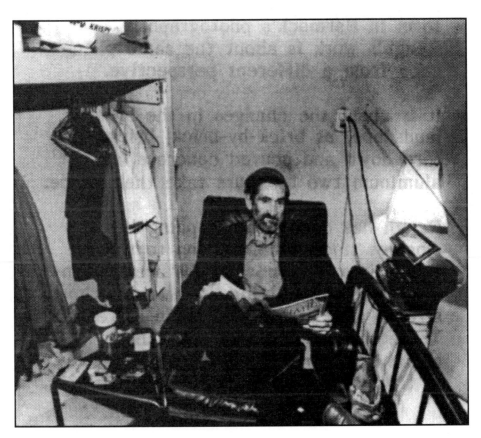

Phil, Hotel Liberty

It's the nicest room I have ever had. I hope I can continue on. I won't make a mess. I have given up sculpture, so there won't be any clay around to get on the carpet.

Thomas Berger, Killing Time

Room and tomb, tomb and womb, womb and room.

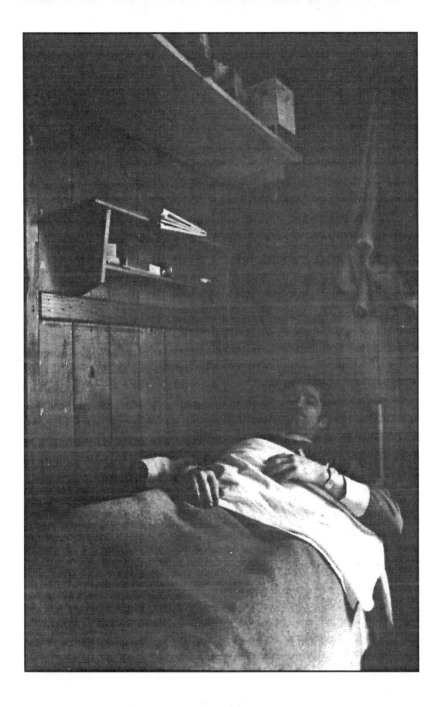

In nightgown and wrap she returned to bed. She lay back against a bank of pillows and imitated the cackling of a turkey. Some women might have considered the possibility that they were going mad. She began to move her head from side to side on the bank of pillows, thus tilting her view of the room from side to side. When she felt giddy, she got out of bed and dropped on to her hands and knees: the carpeted floor was level and still. On the level ground in the free space she was conscious of being happy.

John Berger, G.

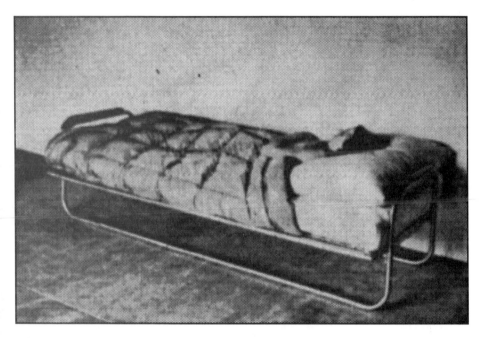

Alvar Aalto, Tubular steel sofa convertible into a bedstead

Accessories

What is this style anyway? It is hard to define. In my opinion the best answer to the question of what stylish is was given by that stout housewife who said, "When there is a lion's head on the night table, and when this same lion's head is present on the sofa, the chest, the beds, the chairs, the washstand, in short, on all objects in the room, then one calls this room stylish."

Adolf Loos, Interiors in the Rotunda

After a day he found Pickett in the room of flies. The air damp and thick. He had to practically sweep the flies off his face and hair.

Don't kill one you bastard or you'll be out, in fact get out'f here, willya.

What the fuck is all this.

I invite them in, ok? If you don't like it get out.

Webb could hardly breathe without one going in his nose or into his mouth. Early evening and the windows closed, no breeze, just Tom Pickett and open food on plates around the room.

Michael Ondaatje, Coming Through Slaughter

Whenever it was possible, George Bush and I had lunch together on Thursdays, when I got a chance to bring him up to date on problems and the administration's current agenda. We looked forward to these private lunches; the White House mess featured Mexican food on Thursdays, since George was from Texas and I was from California.

Madame Monce: "Salope! Salope! How many times have I told you not to squash bugs on the wallpaper? Do you think you've bought the hotel, eh? Why can't you throw them out of the window like everyone else?"

George Orwell, Down and Out in Paris and London

Mulroney on the road during the 1976 leadership race.

For undemocratic reasons and for motives not of State
They arrive at their conclusions — largely inarticulate.
Being void of self-expression they confide their views to none;
But sometimes in a room, one learns why things were done.

Rudyard Kipling, Of the English

A bedroom fit for the heroic pilot of International Squadron, Warner Brothers.

Curtains

Why is there a difference between one window and another, why is there a difference, because the curtain is shorter.

Gertrude Stein, Tender Buttons

Two unequal windows

He was by nature conservative but able also to imagine the worst devices, the capacity for accident in a room — a plum on a table, a child approaching and eating the pit of poison, a man walking into a dark room and before joining his wife in bed brushing loose a paraffin lamp from its bracket. Any room was full of such choreography.

Michael Ondaatje, The English Patient

There was the lamp on the table by the open window. There was the fat green davenport. There was the doorway with the green curtains across it. Never sit with your back to a green curtain. It always turns out badly. Something always happens.

Raymond Chandler, The Lady in the Lake

NYPD evidence photo

Just an image: the young woman who has put herself to death. She is lying on the wooden floor. One of her hands still holds the smoking revolver. On the table a letter, the farewell letter. Is the room in which this is happening of good taste? Who will ask that? It is just a room!

Adolf Loos, Das Andere

A curtain, a curtain which is fastened discloses mourning, this does not mean sparrows or elocution or even a whole preparation, it means that there are ears and very often much more altogether.

Gertrude Stein, Tender Buttons

Orson Welles, Touch of Evil

Who cowered in unshaven rooms in underwear, burning their money in wastebaskets and listening to the Terror through the curtains.

Allen Ginsberg, Howl

When she said something about getting separate rooms, you could see the fear bubbling up inside her like acid.

Gil Brewer, The Red Scarf

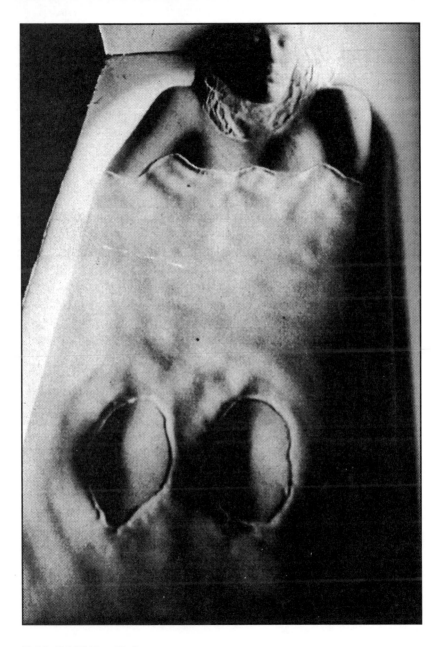

Robin Schiff, Fear Bathroom

It calls to you from the darkness outside the window. The curtains are closed. Everyone you have ever known is assembled there in the falling rain. The suction of feet tramping mud, marching without moving. It opens the window and causes the curtains to move apart. The cold freezes the sweat to your skin. Rain enters horizontally. You try to raise your body to close the window.

Daniel Jones, Obsessions

Carole Conde/Karl Beveridge, Work in Progress

After an epidemic of puerperal fever that claimed 18 victims at the Lyons hospital, workers disinfected the murderous room; this task involved removing layers of old mortar. "As they detached the rubble from the walls and ceiling, the most fetid odor was given off."

Alain Corbin, The Foul and the Fragrant

Rose: Is this room vacant?
Mr. Kidd: Vacant?

Harold Pinter, The Room

Not beyond a certain point.
What point?
Beyond the point where the curtains are drawn back.

John Berger, G.

Ian Carr-Harris, In German

They are buried in the walls. The dead who were murdered and never avenged.

They speak through the rushing of water in the pipes, the knocking of the radiator, the wind that rattles the panes of glass in the window frames.

The plaster cracks and white dust gathers on the floor.

Daniel Jones, Obsessions

Martine Matthews, Dream Homes

Working a room is a risk, no doubt about it.

Susan Roane, How to Work a Room

Simone Forti, See-Saw

She sat on the bed and said, "Cripes!"

I didn't say anything. There was the bed, a straight-backed chair, a paint-peeling, battle-scarred bureau with an empty water pitcher and a pencil on the bare top. There were brown curtains on the window, and the walls were painted blue. There was one lamp by the bed with a frothy pink shade, and the bathroom looked older than the hotel.

She sat there on the bed and I stood by the closed door and it was cold. Finally she got up and went over and peeked out the window, around the shade, and turned with her hands clasped together like she was praying.

Gil Brewer, The Red Scarf

Curtains are rarely well disposed, or well chosen in respect to other decorations. With formal furniture, curtains are out of place; and an extensive volume of drapery of any kind is, under any circumstances, irreconcilable with good taste — the proper quantum, as well as the proper adjustment, depending upon the character of the general effect.

Edgar Allan Poe, Philosophy of Furniture

At the rear of the hallway he floundered through a curtain and stood in a small room. Somewhere before him in the dark people were breeding with rhythmic grunts. He backed out. He pulled at a doorknob. His gorge gave way and the foul liquors in his stomach welled and spewed. He tried to catch it in his hands.

God, he said. He was wiping himself on a curtain. He found a door and entered a room and collapsed in the cool dark. There was a bed there and he tried to crawl under it.

In his stupor he dreamed riots. A window full of glass somewhere collapsed in a crash.

Cormac McCarthy, Suttree

And the silken, sad, uncertain rustling of each purple curtain
Thrilled me — filled me with fantastic terrors never felt before ...

Edgar Allan Poe, The Raven

People's Temple Children's Black Light Discipline Room

What she said made me afraid again, and it was a tangible fear, as if the moment I left her room the burned corpses of half the world would be lying outside the door.

Norman Mailer, The Deer Park

Michael Snow, Cover To Cover

A scream was building in his throat when he saw the beige curtain that separated the room from another one behind it. When a gust of wind ruffled the curtain he did scream.

Now he knew.

He jerked the girl and the old man to their feet and shoved them to the curtain. When they were trembling in front of it, he dragged the counterman over and stationed him beside them. Muttering, "Green door, green door," he paced out five yards, wheeled and squeezed off three perfect head shots. The horrible beige curtain exploded into crimson.

James Ellroy, Because the Night

Fred Zinnemann, The Day of the Jackal

The simplest treatment is often the most charming, but curtains should be full.

Art Begins At Home, The Book of Knowledge Children's Encyclopedia

She turned and walked into her room, leaving the door open. Yevsey remained at the door, trying not to look at the sofa.

"Is he dead, really dead?" he asked in a whisper.

"Yes," answered the woman distinctly.

Then Yevsey turned his head, and glanced indifferently at the little body of his master. Flat and dry it lay upon the sofa as if glued to it. He looked at the corpse, then at Rayissa, and breathed a sigh of relief.

In the corner near the bed the clock on the wall sounded softly and hesitatingly, one stroke, then a second. At each stroke the woman started; she went up to the clock and stopped the halting pendulum with an uncertain hand. She sat down on the bed, her elbows on her knees and her head pressed between her hands. Her hair fell down again, covering her face and hands like a dense, dark curtain.

Barely touching the floor with his toes so as not to break the stern silence, Yevsey went over to Rayissa, gazing at her white round shoulders, and said in a low voice, "It's what he deserved."

"Open the window," said Rayissa gruffly. "Wait a moment. Are you afraid?" she added softly.

"No."

"How is that? You are a timid boy."

"When you are here, I'm not afraid."

"Are you sorry for him?"

"No."

"Open the window."

Maxim Gorky, The Life of a Useless Man

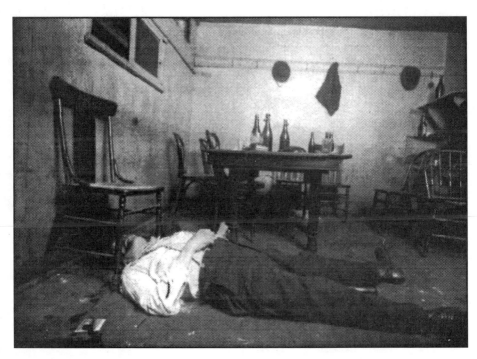

NYPD evidence photo

The room was so still that I could hear it going through my nose, softly, like little curtains rustling.

Raymond Chandler, The High Window

Michael Snow, Cover to Cover

The Fluidity of Rooms

And all that happened after that, in that room, was a dream to Sybil, or a play she watched.

William Gibson and Bruce Sterling, The Difference Engine

Joseph F. Schram, Planning and Remodeling a Bathroom

The Dutch have, perhaps, an indeterminate idea that a curtain is not a cabbage.

Edgar Allan Poe, Philosophy of Furniture

Jim Dine, Black Bathroom #2

The street door was unfastened.

"Party on, perhaps," Sheila said.

"I hear no revelry," I said, and we went in and up the narrow stairs.

The door at the top was ajar. I pushed it open and we went into the room. It was as Jane had seen it, we knew that later. Everything we found was as she described it but for one thing.

John Newton Chance, Three Masks of Death

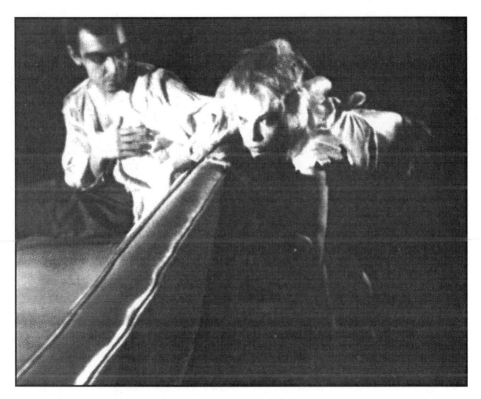

Tom Palazzolo, Caligari's Cure

That night in Lansdowne Crescent, at 8:45, Guy sat on the second sofa in the second drawing-room with a rare second drink and thought: How will I ever know anything in the middle of all this warmth and space, all this supershelter? I want to feel like the trampolinist when he falls back to earth and to gravity. To touch the earth with heaviness. Just to touch it. God expose us, take away our padding and our room.

Martin Amis, London Fields

Marcel Breuer, Isoken wooden armchair

Rushing down, forward and moving off into the depths from column A1 on downward, the staircase, in its increasing explosion, displaces column A1 standing in its path, hurls forward, but now no longer by only the one flight of stairs E1 but like a stroke of lightning in zigzag fashion — E, E1, E2 — hurls forward to the maximum possible extent. In exactly the same way, the system of arches D, while increasing its tendency to plunge into the depths, in the course of having changed the angular contour into a semicircular one breaks with its thrust through this enclosing wall with the barred window and whirls off somewhere in the direction of a general point of descent; and following this example, the solid foundation of the floor vanishes with a roar.

Sergei Eisenstein, Piranesi, or The Fluidity of Forms

Rosemarie Castoro, Roomcracking

"We shouldn't have bought such expensive stuff. It doesn't quite go with the room, does it?"

"Neither do we," she said.

Leonard Cohen, The Favourite Game

The most beautiful rooms I have entered have been empty ones. Warehouses full of light and dust. Empty attics with a view. Plains without trees. I hope to be a pauper by the time I'm thirty.

Yann Martel, The Mirror Machine

... success is alright anyway and any curtain is wholesale. A curtain diminishes and an ample space shows varnish.

Gertrude Stein, Tender Buttons

Ludwig Mies van der Rohe, Tugendhat House

I sit with this room. With the grey walls that darken into corner. And one window with teeth in it. Sit so still you can hear your hair rustle in your shirt. Look away from the window when clouds and other things go by. Thirty-one years old. There are no prizes.

Michael Ondaatje, Coming Through Slaughter

The room made me think of a box — the inside of a huge, rotting packing crate. Four bare walls with the scaly remnants of paper on them like psoriatic skin, bare uncarpeted floor, unshaded bulb hanging from the center of a bare ceiling. The bulb was dark; what light there was came from a low-wattage reading lamp and a wash of red-and-green neon from the hotel's sign that spilled in through a single window. Old iron-framed bed, unpainted nightstand, scarred dresser, straight-backed chair next to the bed and in front of the window, alcove with a sink and toilet and no door, closet that wouldn't be much larger than a coffin.

"Not much, is it," Eddie said.

I didn't say anything.

Bill Pronzini, Souls Burning

Betty Goodwin, Losing Energy

Interiors are no good. As soon as a door closes on a man, he begins to smell and everything he has on him smells too. Body and soul he deteriorates. He rots. It serves us right if people stink. We should have looked after them. We should have taken them out, evicted them, exposed them to the air. All things that stink are indoors.

Celine, Journey to the End of the Night

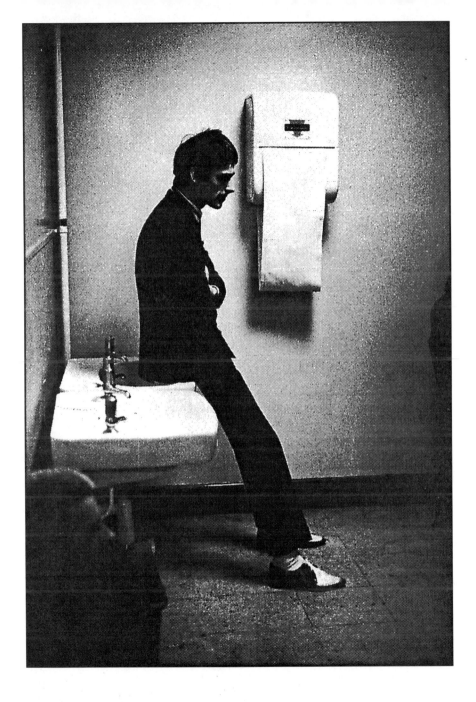

... certainly a room is big enough when it is so empty and the corners are gathered together.

Gertrude Stein, Tender Buttons

I had only to look at my room to know what was happening. The room was a machine that measured my condition: how much of me remained, how much of me was no longer there. I was both perpetrator and witness, both actor and audience in a theater of one. I could follow the progress of my own dismemberment. Piece by piece, I could watch myself disappear.

Paul Auster, Moon Palace

You have now studied your room and decided how you will disguise any defects. The next step is to work out your color scheme.

Art Begins at Home, The Book of Knowledge Children's Encyclopedia

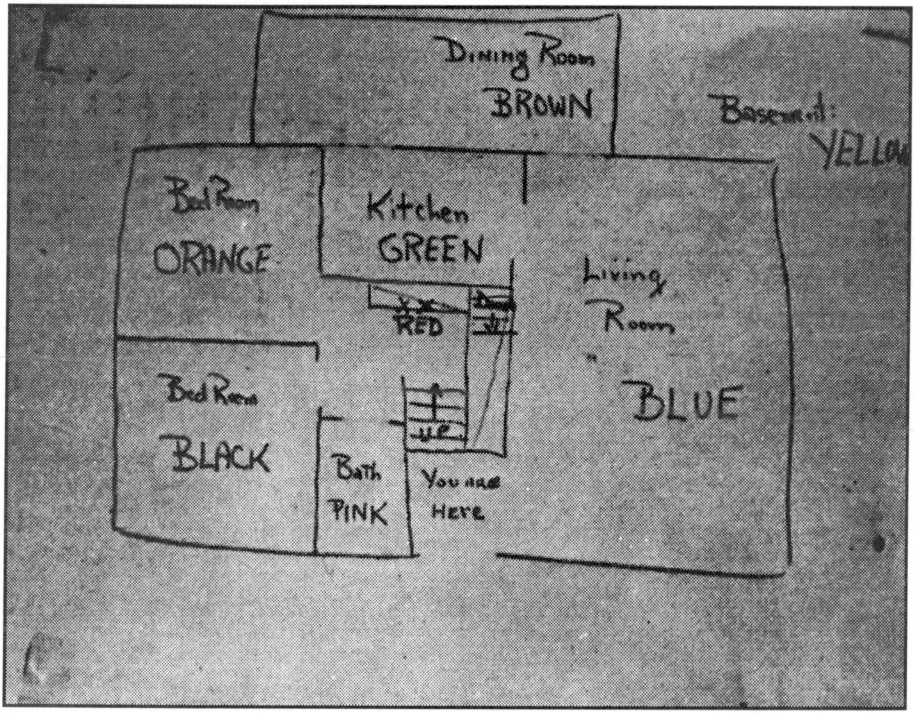

Dining Room
BROWN

Basement:
YELLOW

Bed Room
ORANGE

Kitchen
GREEN

Living
Room
BLUE

RED

Bed Room
BLACK

Bath
PINK

You are
Here

UP

The fire begins with Bellocq positioning his chairs all the way round the room. 17 chairs. Some of which he has borrowed. Then he takes the taper, lights it, stands on a chair, and sets fire to the wallpaper half way up to the ceiling, walks along the path of chairs to continue the flame until he has made a full circle of the room. With great difficulty he steps down and comes back to the centre of the room. The noise is great. Planks cracking beneath the wallpaper in this heat as he stands there silent, as still as possible, trying to formally breathe in the remaining oxygen.

And then the break when he cannot breathe calm and he vomits out smoke and throws himself against the red furniture, against the chairs on fire and he crashes finally into the wall, only there is no wall any more only a fire curtain and he disappears into and through it as if diving through a wave and emerging red on the other side. In an incredible angle. He has expected the wall to be there and his body has prepared itself and his mind has prepared itself so his shape is constricted against an imaginary force looking as if he has come up against an invisible structure in the air.

Then he falls, dissolving out of his pose. Everything has gone wrong. The wall is not there to catch or hide him. Nothing is there to clasp him into a certainty.

Michael Ondaatje, Coming Through Slaughter

Rose: Mr. Kidd, what did they mean about this room?
Mr. Kidd: What room?

Harold Pinter, The Room

The most important factor here is that you understand that a room is a matter of opinion.

Fran Lebowitz, A Manual: Training for Landlords

When we were outside the door I asked, "Is this a restaurant?"

She just laughed and jangled the key and fumbled with the lock. It was not that she was unmechanical, but rather that she was too vain to wear her glasses. At last the key turned and she pushed the door open.

"Do you like it?"

I stepped inside and looked around.

"Is it a living room?"

Paul Theroux, My Secret History

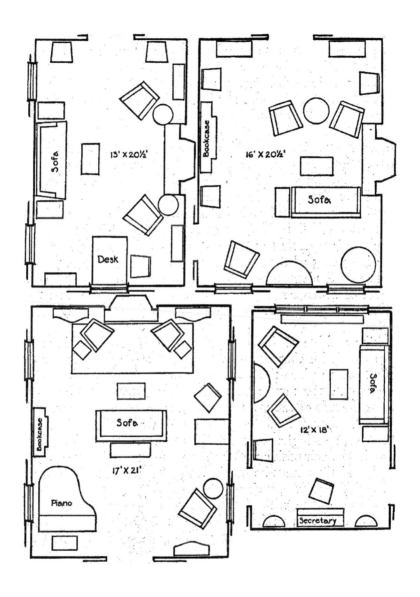

Examples of furniture arrangements for living rooms of various shapes and sizes.

Then what about rooms, wasn't every room the same, hadn't he known what it would be like, weren't all the rooms they passed exactly the same, wherever a woman was stretched out, even a forest was a glass room.

Leonard Cohen, The Favourite Game

I went through the room again, looking for more details that might mean something.

James Ellroy, Clandestine

A room in Gropius ' house at the Weissenhof, 1927

No eye-glasses are rotten, no window is useless.

Gertrude Stein, Tender Buttons

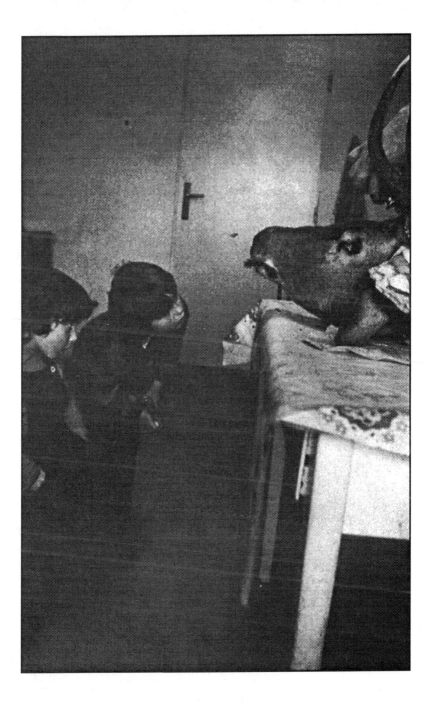

Finally he gave up inventing anything but impracticable rooms, revolving rooms, kaleidoscopic interiors, adjustable scenery for the soul, and his ideas grew steadily more and more insubstantial.

Robert Musil, The Man Without Qualities

The other day I wrote down the following wish: "When passing a house, to be pulled in through the ground-floor window by a rope tied around one's neck and to be hauled up, bloody and ragged, through all the ceilings, furniture, walls, and attics, without consideration, as if by a person who is paying no attention, until the empty noose, dropping the last shreds of me when breaking through the roof tiles, appears on the roof.

Franz Kafka, Letters to Felice

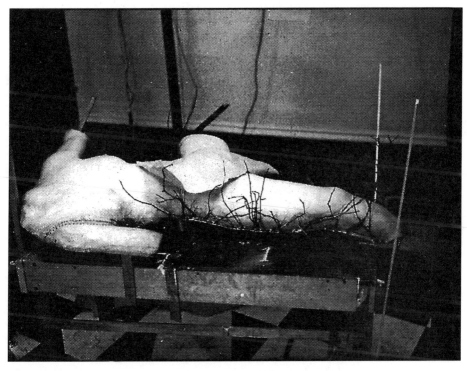

Marcel Duchamp, from Manual of Instructions for Étant Donnés

The world has shrunk to the size of this room, and for as long as it takes him to understand it, he must stay where he is. Only one thing is certain: he cannot be anywhere until he is here.

Paul Auster, The Invention of Solitude

Russell Spanner, 253 pounds, stands on 20-pound coffee table.

"Do you like what I've done with the room?"

The room, the sole one in the hut, looked no different to Pilar. Shelves, none any deeper than two inches, lined the walls from floor to ceiling, most of them crooked and all of them populated by a strange array of knickknacks — little colored jars, tiny stick dolls, peculiar jewelry, toy automobiles, plastic snakes, tins of gray powder. Her grandmother had once made her living predicting the future, and Pilar knew that many of the items were props she had used, but they were such odd props — scraps of fabric, surprises from Cracker Jacks, chips of broken glass, tabs from beer cans — silly and inconsequential things.

"I can't see that you've changed anything," Pilar told her.

Maria walked to the bed and sat beside her. "The pillow used to be at this end," she said. "I moved it up there." She pointed to the other end of the bed and the crumpled feather pillow. "Now, when I lie down, the room is completely turned around.

Robert Boswell, The Geography of Desire

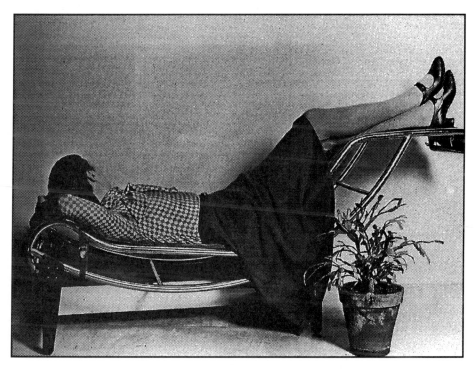

Le Corbusier and Charlotte Perriand, Chaise-Lounge, 1928-29

The whole arrangement is established. The end of which is that there is a suggestion, a suggestion that there can be a different whiteness to a wall. This was thought.

Gertrude Stein, Tender Buttons

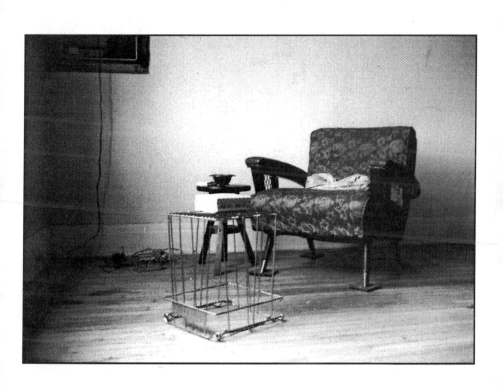

I got up on my feet and went over to the bowl in the corner and threw cold water on my face. After a little while I felt a little better, but very little. I needed a drink, I needed a lot of life insurance, I needed a vacation, I needed a home in the country. What I had was a coat, a hat and a gun. I put them on and went out of the room.

Raymond Chandler, Farewell My Lovely

Sources

Sources are listed in order of appearance.

Texts

Don DeLillo, White Noise, New York: Penguin Books, 1984, p. 306.

Cormac McCarthy, Suttree, New York: Random House, 1979, p.77.

Susan Kent, Analyzing Activity Areas: An Ethnoarcheological Study of the Use of Space, Albuquerque: University of New Mexico Press, 1984.

Eldon Garnet, I Shot Mussolini, Toronto: Summerhill Press, p. 85.

Michael Ondaatje, Coming Through Slaughter. Toronto: House of Anansi, 1976, p. 146.

Raymond Chandler, The Lady in the Lake (1943), from The Raymond Chandler Omnibus, New York: Random House, 1975.

Franz Kafka, The Metamorphosis (1915), from The Basic Kafka, New York: Simon and Schuster, 1979.

Peter Greenaway , 26 Bathrooms (video).

Eric McCormack, The Paradise Motel, London: Collins Publishing, 1989, p.99.

DeLillo, White Noise, p.306.

F. Earle Barcus, Romper Room: An Analysis, Boston: Boston University, 1971.

B.W. Powe, Outage: A Journey Into Electric City, Toronto: Random House, 1989, p.126.

George Orwell, Keep The Aspidistra Flying (1936), London: Penguin, 1987, p. 28.

Norman Mailer, Barbary Shore, New York: Signet Books, 1951, p.68.

Walter Benjamin, "Paris, Capital of the Nineteenth Century" (1955), Reflections, New York: Schocken Books, 1986, p. 155.

Thomas Fuller, The Holy State and the Profane State (1642), The Oxford Dictionary of Quotations, Oxford University Press, 1979.

Harold Pinter, The Room, from Plays: One, Methuen, 1976.

Daniel Jones, Obsessions, Stratford, Ontario: The Mercury Press, 1992, p. 64.

Fran Lebowitz, "A Manual: Training For Landlords" from The Fran Lebowitz Reader, New York: Random House, 1994, p. 43.

Robert Boswell, The Geography of Desire, New York: Harper Collins, 1989,

p. 13.

Maxim Gorky, The Life of a Useless Man (1917), London: Penguin Books, 1981, p.99.

Philip Larkin, The Old Fools, The Oxford Dictionary of Quotations, Oxford University Press, 1979.

Adolf Loos, "Interiors in the Rotunda," Spoken into the Void: Collected Essays, 1897-1900, Cambridge, Mass.: MIT Press, 1982, p.24.

Charles Bukowski, Notes of a Dirty Old Man, San Francisco: City Lights Books, 1973, p.116.

Franz Kafka, Description of a Struggle, from The Basic Kafka, New York: Simon & Schuster, 1979.

Pinter, The Room.

Robert Musil, The Man Without Qualities (1930), London: Pan Books, 1979.

The Holy Bible, Luke, 22:12.

Julian Barnes, Talking It Over, Toronto: Random House, 1991, p.125.

DeLillo, White Noise, p. 306.

Leonard Cohen, The Favourite Game, Toronto, McClelland and Stewart, 1963, p. 77.

Paul Theroux, My Secret History, London: Penguin, 1989, p. 122.

McCarthy, Suttree, p. 176.

Mailer, Barbary Shore, p. 39.

Charles Bukowski, Women, Santa Rosa: Black Sparrow Press, 1992, p. 22.

Susan Roane, How To Work A Room, New York, Business Books, 1986.

DeLillo, White Noise, p. 306.

Raymond Chandler, The Big Sleep (1939), p.96.

Martin Amis, London Fields, London: Penguin, 1989, p. 61.

Pinter, The Room.

Powe, Outage, p. 50, 54.

Powe, Outage, p.61.

Barcus, Romper Room.

Powe, Outage, p. 51, 54.

Don DeLillo, Mao II, New York: Penguin, 1991, p. 161.

Paul Auster, Ghosts, New York: Penguin, 1986, p. 66.

Wyndham Lewis, source unknown.

Paul Auster, The Invention of Solitude, New York: Avon Books, 1982, p. 89.

Virginia Woolf, A Room of One's Own (1929), London, Harper

Collins, 1994, p. 95.

Fyodor Dostoyevsky, Crime and Punishment, Harmondsworth: Penguin, 1981, p.430-431.

Edgar Allan Poe, "The Masque of the Red Death," The Portable Poe, Harmondsworth: Penguin, 1980, p. 284.

Bukowski, Dirty Old Man, p. 33.

Thomas Pynchon, V., Philadelphia: J.B. Lippincott, 1963, p. 284-5.

Powe, Outage, p.146.

Barcus, Romper Room.

DeLillo, Mao II, p. 132.

Auster, Solitude, p. 98-100.

Nurse's notes, St. Elizabeth's Hospital (1950's), re: Ezra Pound. From Humphrey Carpenter, A Serious Character - The Life of Ezra Pound, New York: Bantam Doubleday Dell, 1988, p.778.

Bukowski, Dirty Old Man, p. 27.

Pinter, The Room.

Attributed to Hegel by Edgar Allan Poe, "Philosophy of Furniture," Collected Works, v.II, Harvard University Press, 1978, p. 495.

Attributed to Pascal by Auster, Solitude, p.76.

Auster, Solitude, p. 143-144.

Auster, Solitude, p.160.

Gustave Flaubert, letter, 1845, from Henri Troyat, Flaubert, New York: Viking Penuin, 1992, p.53.

Thomas Berger, Killing Time, New York: Dell Publishing, 1967, p. 133.

Auster, Solitude.

John Berger, G., Harmondsworth: Penguin, 1972, p. 105.

Loos, Interiors in the Rotunda, p. 23.

Ondaatje, Coming Through Slaughter, p. 70.

George Orwell, Down and Out in Paris and London (1933), New York: Harcourt Brace Jovanovich, 1961, p. 5.

Rudyard Kipling, Of The English, The Oxford Dictionary of Quotations, Oxford University Press, 1979.

Gertrude Stein, Tender Buttons (1914), from Selected Writings, New York: Random House, 1990, p. 503.

Michael Ondaatje, The English Patient, Toronto: Random House, 1992, p. 111.

Chandler, The Lady in the Lake, p.595.

Adolf Loos, Das Andere, no. 1 (1903), from Beatriz Colomina, Privacy and
    Publicity - Modern Architecture as Mass Media, Cambridge: MIT
    Press, 1994, p. 252.
Stein, Tender Buttons, p. 505.
Allan Ginsberg, Howl, San Francisco: City Lights Books, 1956.
Gil Brewer, "The Red Scarf" (1958), Dark Crimes, Ed Gorman, ed., New
    York: Carroll and Graf, 1991, p. 132.
Jones, Obsessions, p. 14.
Alain Corbin, The Foul and the Fragrant, publisher and date unknown.
Pinter, The Room.
Berger, G.
Jones, Obsessions, p. 83.
Roane, How To Work A Room.
Brewer, The Red Scarf, p. 132.
Poe, Philosophy of Furniture, p. 497.
McCarthy, Suttree, p. 78.
Edgar Allan Poe, "The Raven," The Portable Poe, Harmondsworth: Penguin,
    1980, p. 618.
Norman Mailer, The Deer Park, New York: Signet Books, 1956.
James Ellroy, Because The Night, New York: Avon Books, 1984, p. 2.
"Art Begins At Home," The Book of Knowledge Children's Encyclopedia,
    Toronto: Grolier, 1955, v. 16, p. 5714.
Gorky, Useless Man, p. 70.
Chandler, The High Window, (1942), from The Raymond Chandler
    Omnibus, New York: Random House, 1975.
William Gibson and Bruce Sterling, The Difference Engine, New York:
    Bantam Books, 1991, p. 66.
Poe, Philosophy of Furniture, p. 496.
John Newton Chance, Three Masks of Death, New York: Lion Books, 1964.
Amis, London Fields, p. 38.
Sergei Eisenstein, "Piranesi, or The Fluidity of Forms," from Manfredo
    Tafuri, The Sphere and the Labyrinth: Avant-Gardes and
    Architecture from Piranesi to the 1970s, Cambridge: MIT Press, p. 69.
Cohen, Favourite Game, p.81.
Yann Martel, "The Mirror Machine," The Facts behind the Helsinki
    Roccamatios and other stories, Toronto: Alfred A. Knopf, 1993, p. 224.

Stein, Tender Buttons, p. 504.

Ondaatje, Coming Through Slaughter, p. 156.

Bill Pronzini, "Souls Burning", Dark Crimes, p. 56.

Louis-Ferdinand Céline, Journey To The End Of The Night (1934), New
York: New Directions Books, 1983, p. 308.

Stein, Tender Buttons, p. 506.

Paul Auster, Moon Palace, New York: Viking Penguin, 1989.

Art Begins At Home, Book of Knowledge, v. 16, p.5724.

Ondaatje, Coming Through Slaughter, p. 67.

Pinter, The Room.

Lebowitz, A Manual: Training For Landlords.

Theroux, Secret History, p. 131.

Cohen, The Favourite Game, p.182.

James Ellroy, Clandestine, New York: Avon Books, 1982, p. 49.

Stein, Tender Buttons, p. 501.

Musil, The Man Without Qualities, v.1, p. 17.

Franz Kafka, Letters To Felice, from The Basic Kafka, p. 282.

Auster, Solitude, p. 79.

Boswell, The Geography of Desire.

Stein, Tender Buttons, p. 499.

Chandler, Farewell, My Lovely, p. 283.

Photographs

Photo by Tom Ballard. Copyright Tom Ballard/EKM Nepenthe.

NYPD evidence photo, c. 1915, from Luc Sante, Low Life - Lures and
   Snares of Old New York, New York: Random House, 1991, p. 124.

Kent, Analyzing Activity Areas.

From Kenneth Anger, Hollywood Babylon, London: Arrow Books, 1975.

Photo by Adrian Blackwell.

Village Voice, Oct. 9, 1990, uncredited.

Jules Amar, Filer with respiratory apparatus, ca. 1912, from Jules Amar, Le
   Moteur humain et les bases scientifiques du travail professionnel,
   Paris, 1914. (Anson Rabinbach, The Human Motor — Energy,
   Fatigue, and the Origins of Modernity, New York: Basic Books,
   1990)

Joseph F. Schram, Planning and Remodeling a Bathroom, Toronto: Coles,
   1978.

Author's collection.

K. Luchesskoy, Housing To Fit The Need, Moscow: Novosti Publishing
   House, 1976.

Simone Forti, Handbook in Motion, Halifax: Nova Scotia College of Art and
   Design, 1974, p. 43.

Luchesskoy, Housing To Fit The Need.

Furniture by L. Reich, Berlin, 1931, from Leonardo Benevolo, History of
   Modern Architecture, Cambridge: MIT Press, 1977, v. 2, p. 489.

Photo by Rob Kovitz.

Photo by Mary Ellen Mark, The Photo Essay, Washington: Smithsonian
   Institution Press, 1990.

Vasari Junior, La Pietra, anteroom with frescoed walls.

Author's collection.

Toronto Globe and Mail, Dec. 22, 1993.

Author's collection.

Alvar Aalta, Paimio sanitorium, 1929-31, from Benevolo, Modern
   Architecture, p.618.

Photo by Ken Hayman, from Ken Hayman, The World's Family, New York:
   G.P. Putnam's Sons, 1983, p. 161.

Photo by Wallace Kirkland, 1952. From Richard Lacayo and George Russell,
   Eyewitness - 150 Years of Photojournalism, New York: Time, p. 154.

Toney W. Merritt, film still from The Shadow Line, 1986, from
   Cinematograph, v. 2, p. 88.

Matthew Geller, Difficulty Swallowing - A Medical Chronicle, New York: Works Press, 1981.

Photo by Raymond Pronier, from Photographies Magazine, p. 75.

Author's collection.

Lewis Klahr, film still from Deep Fishtank, Too, 1987, from Cinematograph, v. 3, p. 102.

Photo by Massimo Bacigalupo, from Carpenter, A Serious Character .

Ralph Levy, director, film still from Bedtime Story, 1964.

Billy Wilder, director, film still from Double Indemnity, Paramount, 1944.

Photo by Jean Mohr, from John Berger and Jean Mohr, A Seventh Man, Cambridge: Granta Books, 1989, p. 174.

Jean-Jacques Lequeu, Design of a Bed for the Beglierbey of Rumelia, from Phillippe Duboy, Lequeu - An Architectural Enigma, Cambridge: MIT Press, 1987, p. 28.

Photo by Rob Kovitz.

Maurice Defrène, Woman's Bedroom, Exposition des Arts Décoratifs, Paris, 1925, from AA Files 15, Summer 1987, p. 4.

From Ernest A. Bell, Fighting the Traffic in Young Girls, or War on the White Slave Trade, 1911.

1974 World Book Year Book, Chicago: Field Enterprises Educational Corporation, 1974.

Author's collection.

Marcel Breuer, Man's Room, Salon des Artistes Décorateurs, Paris, 1930, from AA Files 15, p. 10.

From Anger, Hollywood Babylon, p. 124.

Photo by Brassaï, from Brassaï, The Secret Paris of the 30's, New York: Random House, 1976.

Tonya Harding and Jeff Gillooly, still from home video, from Penthouse, September 1994, p. 121.

Luchesskoy, Housing to Fit the Need.

Sorel Cohen, After Bacon/Muybridge, coupled figures/shoulder toss.

Bruce Nauman, Come Piece, 1969, from Ursula Meyer, Conceptual Art, New York: E.P. Dutton, 1972, p. 189, New York.

Albrecht Durer, Saint Jerome in His Cell, 1514, from Elizabeth Ripley, Durer, Philadelphia: J.B. Lippincott Company, 1958, p. 53

Photo by Rob Kovitz.

Photo by V. Vale from RE/Search, no.6/7, 1983, p.14.

Author's collection.

Julien Duvivier, director, film still from Flesh and Fantasy, Universal, 1943.

From "Art Begins at Home," The Book of Knowledge Children's Encyclopedia.

Alberto Giacometti, Annette, sitting, 1957.

Derek Jarman, film still from The Last of England, 1987.

Author's collection.

Kika Thorne, film still from Goodbye Suicide Girl.

Douglas Sirk, director, film still from All That Heaven Allows, Universal, 1955.

Photo by Yoichi Okamoto of J. Edgar Hoover, from Curt Gentry, J. Edgar Hoover - The Man and the Secrets, New York: W.W. Norton, 1991.

Photo by Melitta Mew, the interior of a cell at the Nuremburg jail, 1945. From Ann Tusa and John Tusa, The Nuremburg Trial, New York: Atheneum, 1984.

Photo by Jean Mohr, from A Seventh Man, p. 191.

Photo by Raymond Depardon, 1979, from Eyewitness, p. 155

Vito Acconci, Step Piece, 1970, photo by Kathy Dillon, from Ursula Meyer, Conceptual Art, p. 2.

From Ray Monk, Ludwig Wittgenstein - The Duty of Genius, London: Vintage, 1990.

Author's collection.

Vincent Van Gogh, The Bedroom

Photo by Gaston Bergeret, from Photographies Magazine, p.57.

Photo by Richard Bermack, Phil, Hotel Liberty, from Left Curve, no. 12, 1987-8, p.84.

Photo of Jackson Pollock, from Steven Naifeh and Gregory White Smith, Jackson Pollock - An American Saga, New York: Harper Collins, 1989, p. 666.

Photo by Jean Mohr, from A Seventh Man, p. 85.

Alvar Aalto, Tubular steel sofa convertible into a bedstead, 1932, from Siegfried Giedion, Mechanization Takes Command - A contribution to anonymous history (1948), New York: W.W. Norton, 1969, p. 430.

Author's collection.

Photo by White House photographers, Ronald Reagan - An American Life, New York: Simon and Schuster, 1990.

Canada Wide Photo, from John Sawatsky, Mulroney - The Politics of Ambition, Toronto: Macfarlane Walter and Ross, 1991, after p. 306.

Lothar Mendes, director, film still from International Squadron, Warner,

1941, from Laurence Leamer, Make Believe - The Story of Nancy
and Ronald Reagan, New York: Harper and Row, 1983, p. 121
"Art Begins At Home,", The Book of Knowledge Children's Encyclopedia, p.
5718.
Author's collection.
NYPD evidence photo, c. 1915, from Luc Sante, Low Life, p. 209.
"Art Begins At Home," p. 5717.
Orson Welles, director, film still from Touch of Evil, Universal, 1958.
From Kenneth Anger, Hollywood Babylon.
Robin Schiff, Fear Bathroom, photo by Lloyd Hamrol, from Judy Chicago,
Through The Flower.
Carole Conde and Karl Beveridge, Work in Progress, 1980-1, from Left
Curve, p. 46.
Photo by Rob Kovitz.
"Art Begins At Home," p. 5715.
Ian Carr-Harris, In German, 1982.
Martine Matthews, "Dream Homes" (invivo exploratory), 1987, from C
Magazine, 15, Sept. 1987.
Simone Forti, See Saw, from Handbook in Motion, p. 41.
Photo by Rob Kovitz.
"Art Begins At Home," p. 5715.
From 1974 World Book Year Book.
Photo by Jim Jocoy, from RE/Search, p. 77.
Michael Snow, Cover To Cover, Halifax: The Press of the Nova Scotia
College of Art and Design.
Fred Zinnemann, film still from The Day of The Jackal, Universal, 1973.
"Art Begins At Home," p. 5716.
NYPD evidence photo, from Luc Sante, Low Life, p. 124.
Michael Snow, Cover To Cover.
Schram, Planning and Remodeling a Bathroom, p. 111.
Jim Dine, Black Bathroom #2, 1962, Art Gallery of Ontario.
Tom Palazzolo, film still from Caligari's Cure, 1982, from Cinematograph, v.
3, p. 142.
Marcel Breuer, Isoken wooden armchair, from Benevolo, Modern
Architecture, p. 590.
Rosemarie Castoro, Roomcracking, 1969, from Conceptual Art, p.104.
Photo by Adrian Blackwell.
Photo by Rob Kovitz.

Ludwig Mies van der Rohe, Tugendhat House, 1930, from Benevolo, Modern Architecture, p. 503.

Photo by Jim Allen of Bill Grove, from Saturday Night, Feb. 95.

Betty Goodwin, Losing Energy.

Photo by Penny Smith, from Paul Honeyford, The Jam - The Modern World by Numbers, London: Eel Pie Publishing, 1980, p. 73.

Photo by Mary Ellen Mark.

Author's collection.

From Family Circle Do-It-Yourself Encyclopedia, Vol. 11, p. 1548.

Photo by Coum Transmissions, from RE/Search, p. 73.

Photo by Pennie Smith, from Honeyford, The Jam, p. 71.

Author's collection.

From Sherrill Whiton, Elements of Interior Design and Decoration, Chicago: J.B. Lippincott Company, 1951.

Photo by Nan Goldin, from Henry Horenstein, Color Photography, Boston: Little, Brown and Company, 1995, p. 135.

Walter Gropius, House, 1927, from Benevolo, Modern Architecure, p. 428.

Photo by Jindrich Streit, from Granta 32, Spring 1990, p. 87.

Photo by Rob Kovitz.

Marcel Duchamp, from Manual of Instructions for Étant Donnés, Philadelphia Museum of Art, 1987.

Photo of Russell Spanner, The Globe and Mail, 12 January 1954, from Robert Fones, A Spanner in the Works - The Furniture of Russell Spanner, 1950-1953, Toronto: The Power Plant, 1990.

Le Corbusier and Charlotte Perriand, Chaise-Lounge, 1928-29, from AA Files, 15, p. 3.

Photo by Rob Kovitz.

Author's collection.

Permissions

Other titles from Insomniac Press:

The War In Heaven by Kent Nussey

The War In Heaven collects the latest work from Kent Nussey. A unique blend of the stark realism of Raymond Carver and the Iyrical precision of Russell Banks, Nussey's writing levels the mythologies of an urban paradise with fictions that are humorous but dark, touching and   dangerous. In this book nothing is sacred, secure, or safe. Comprised of seven stories and a novella, *The War in Heaven* explores the human capacity for desire and destruction in a world where everything   condenses beyond metaphor into organic connection. For Nussey love is the catalyst, creating the currents which sweep over his complex and provocative characters, and carry the reader to the brink of personal and historical apocalypse.

5 1/4" x 8 1/4" • 192 pages • trade paperback withflaps • isbn 1-895837-42-1

Canada $18.99/U.S. $13.99/U.K. £10.99

Dying for Veronica by Matthew Remski

A love story of bizarre proportions, Matthew Remski's first novel is set in Toronto. *Dying for Veronica* is a gritty and mysterious book,   narrated by a man haunted by a twisted and unhappy childhood and obsessed with the sister he loves. This shadowy past explodes into an even more psychologically disturbing present — an irresistible quest and a longing that can not be denied. Remski's prose is beautiful, provocative, poetic: rich with the dark secrets and intricacies of Catholic mythology as it collides with, and is subsumed by, North American culture.

5 1/4" x 8 1/4" • 224 pages • trade paperback withflaps • isbn 1-895837-40-5

Canada $18.99/U.S. $14.99/U.K. £10.99

Carnival: a Scream In High Park reader edited by Peter McPhee

One evening each July an open-air literary festival is held in Toronto's High Park. It is a midway of diverse voices joined in celebration of poetry and story telling. Audiences exceeding 1,200 people gather under the oak trees to hear both well known and emerging writers from across the country, such as, Lynn Crosbie, Claire Harris, Steven Heighton, Nicole Brossard, Nino Ricci, Al Purdy, Susan Musgrave, Leon Rooke, Christopher Dewdney, Barbara Gowdy, bill bissett... This book collects the work (much of it new and previously unpublished) from the 48 writers who have performed at Scream in

High Park in its first three years.

5 1/4" x 8 1/4" • 216 pages • trade paperback withflaps • isbn 1-895837-38-3
Canada $18.99/U.S. $14.99/U.K. £10.99

What Passes for Love by Stan Rogal

What Passes for Love is a collection of short stories which show the dynamics of male-female relationships. These ten short stories by Stan Rogal resonate with many aspects of the mating rituals of men and women: paranoia, obsession, voyeurism, and assimilation. Stan Rogal's first collection of stories, *What Passes for Love*, is an intriguing search through many relationships, and the emotional turmoil within them. Stan's writing reflects the honesty and unsentimentality,   previously seen in his two books of poetry and published stories. Throughout *What Passes for Love* are paintings by Kirsten Johnson.

5 1/4" x 8 1/4" • 144 pages • trade paperback • isbn 1-895837-34-0
Canada $14.99/U.S. $12.99/U.K. £8.99

Beneath the Beauty by Phlip Arima

Beneath the Beauty is Phlip Arima's first collection of poetry. His work is gritty and rhythmic, passionate and uncompromising. His writing reveals themes like love, life on the street and addiction. Arima has a terrifying clarity of vision in his portrayal of contemporary life. Despite the cruelties inflicted and endured by his characters, he is able to find a compassionate element even in the bleakest of circumstances. Arima has a similar aesthetic to Charles Bukowski, but there is a sense of hope and dark romanticism throughout his work. Phlip Arima is a   powerful poet and storyteller, and his writing is not for the faint of heart.

5 1/4" x 8 1/4" • 80 pages • trade paperback • isbn 1-895837-36-7
Canada $11.99/U.S. $9.99/U.K. £7.99

Insomniac Press • 378 Delaware Ave., Toronto, Ontario, Canada • M6H 2T8
phone: (416) 536-4308 • fax: (416) 588-4198 • email: insomna@pathcom.com

Acknowledgements

Thanks to the following people for their support and encouragement of Treyf:

Mark Berest, Adrian Blackwell, Andy Filarski, Ken Hayes, Bernice Iarocci, Barry Isenor, Beth Kapusta, Marie-Paule Macdonald, Marina Polosa, Andrew Power, Kati Rubinyi, Kika Thorne, Chris Vlcek

Stan Bevington, Brian Boigon, Linda Eerme, Rick Haldenby, Dan Hoffman, Robert Jan Van Pelt, Alexander Pilis, Larry Richards, Kelly Rude, Paul Syme

special thanks on this one to Mike O'Connor.

Room Behavior is the fourth in a series of evocative, wry and enigmatic compilation books by Rob Kovitz. His previous titles include Pig City Model Farm; Death Wish, Starring Charles Bronson, Architect; Games Oligopolists Play; all published by Treyf Books. Kovitz is also an architect and a builder, and currently lives in Gimli, Manitoba.